FOURTH of JULY

By EMMA CARLSON BERNE
Illustrations by LUKE FLOWERS
Music by JOSEPH FAISON IV

CANTATA
LEARNING

WWW.CANTATALEARNING.COM

CANTATA LEARNING

Published by Cantata Learning
1710 Roe Crest Drive
North Mankato, MN 56003
www.cantatalearning.com

Library of Congress Cataloging-in-Publication Data
Names: Berne, Emma Carlson, author. | Flowers, Luke, illustrator.
Title: Fourth of July / by Emma Carlson Berne ; illustrated by Luke Flowers
 ; music by Joseph Faison IV.
Description: North Mankato, MN : Cantata Learning, [2018] | Series: Holidays
 in rhythm and rhyme | Includes bibliographical references. | Audience:
 Ages 5-7. | Audience: K-3.
Identifiers: LCCN 2017017519 (print) | LCCN 2017017938 (ebook) | ISBN
 9781684101566 (ebook) | ISBN 9781684101252 (hardcover : alk. paper) | ISBN
 9781684101924 (pbk. : alk. paper)
Subjects: LCSH: Fourth of July--Juvenile literature. | Fourth of July
 celebrations--Juvenile literature.
Classification: LCC E286 (ebook) | LCC E286 .B47 2018 (print) | DDC
 394.2634--dc23
LC record available at https://lccn.loc.gov/2017017519

Book design and art direction, Tim Palin Creative
Editorial direction, Kellie M. Hultgren
Music direction, Elizabeth Draper
Music arranged and produced by Joseph Faison IV

Printed in the United States of America in North Mankato, Minnesota.
122017   0378CGS18

ACCESS THE MUSIC!

SCAN CODE WITH MOBILE APP

CANTATALEARNING.COM

TIPS TO SUPPORT LITERACY AT HOME

WHY READING AND SINGING WITH YOUR CHILD IS SO IMPORTANT

Daily reading with your child leads to increased academic achievement. Music and songs, specifically rhyming songs, are a fun and easy way to build early literacy and language development. Music skills correlate significantly with both phonological awareness and reading development. Singing helps build vocabulary and speech development. And reading and appreciating music together is a wonderful way to strengthen your relationship.

READ AND SING EVERY DAY!

TIPS FOR USING CANTATA LEARNING BOOKS AND SONGS DURING YOUR DAILY STORY TIME

1. As you sing and read, point out the different words on the page that rhyme. Suggest other words that rhyme.

2. Memorize simple rhymes such as Itsy Bitsy Spider and sing them together. This encourages comprehension skills and early literacy skills.

3. Use the questions in the back of each book to guide your singing and storytelling.

4. Read the included sheet music with your child while you listen to the song. How do the music notes correlate to the words of the song?

5. Sing along on the go and at home. Access music by scanning the QR code on each Cantata book, or by using the included CD. You can also stream or download the music for free to your computer, smartphone, or mobile device.

Devoting time to daily reading shows that you are available for your child. Together, you are building language, literacy, and listening skills.

Have fun reading and singing!

On July 4, 1776, **colonists** living in America made an important **announcement**. They would not be ruled by the king of England anymore. They would create a new, free nation: the United States. So people call the Fourth of July the birthday of the United States. Sometimes this summer holiday is called Independence Day.

On the Fourth of July, people in the United States remember that they are free. They watch parades and fireworks. They have picnics. The Fourth of July is a day for having fun *and* for remembering. Let's sing about the Fourth of July together!

Grab a flag, the parade is coming!

The drums are banging, the flutes are humming.

Floats and fire trucks, here they are.

The mayor waves from a fancy car.

On July the Fourth we sing our song
about the war fought hard and long.

We sing freedom, we sing out loud,
all together, we sing out proud.

The sun is high, it's time to eat!
Here's a blanket, take a seat.

Hot dogs grilling, burgers too.
Plenty of Popsicles, red, white, and blue!

On July the Fourth, we sing our song about the war fought hard and long.

We sing freedom, we sing out loud, all together, we sing out proud.

The sun is down, let's hear the band.
Tap our feet and clap our hands.

A **bugler** plays her golden horn.
A tune from when our nation was born.

On July the Fourth, we sing our song
about the war fought hard and long.

We sing freedom, we sing out loud,
all together, we sing out proud.

Crash! Boom! Bang! Look at the sky, fireworks **exploding** up so high.

"What a **dazzling** show!" we say. We're glad to be free upon this day.

On July the Fourth, we sing our song
about the war fought hard and long.

We sing freedom, we sing out loud,
all together, we sing out proud.

SONG LYRICS
Fourth of July

Grab a flag, the parade is coming!
The drums are banging, the flutes are humming.
Floats and fire trucks, here they are.
The mayor waves from a fancy car.

On July the Fourth, we sing our song
about the war fought hard and long.
We sing freedom, we sing out loud,
all together, we sing out proud.

The sun is high, it's time to eat!
Here's a blanket, take a seat.
Hot dogs grilling, burgers too.
Plenty of Popsicles, red, white, and blue!

On July the Fourth, we sing our song
about the war fought hard and long.
We sing freedom, we sing out loud,
all together, we sing out proud.

The sun is down, let's hear the band.
Tap our feet and clap our hands.
A bugler plays her golden horn.
A tune from when our nation was born.

On July the Fourth, we sing our song
about the war fought hard and long.
We sing freedom, we sing out loud,
all together, we sing out proud.

Crash! Boom! Bang! Look at the sky,
fireworks exploding up so high.
"What a dazzling show!" we say.
We're glad to be free upon this day.

On July the Fourth, we sing our song
about the war fought hard and long.
We sing freedom, we sing out loud,
all together, we sing out proud.

Fourth of July

Jazz
Joseph Faison IV

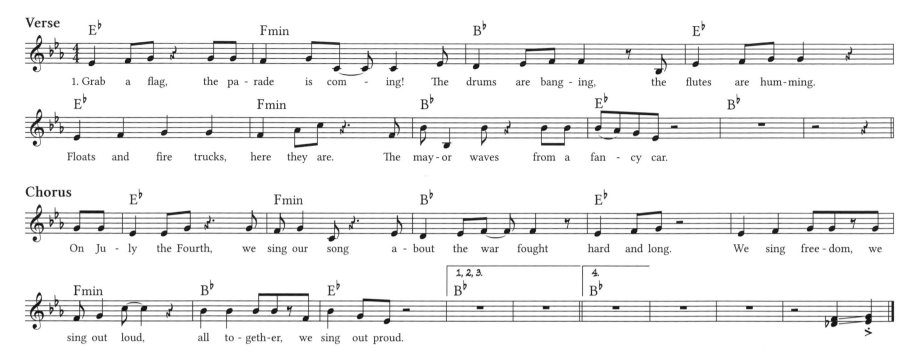

Verse

1. Grab a flag, the pa-rade is com - ing! The drums are bang - ing, the flutes are hum-ming.

Floats and fire trucks, here they are. The may - or waves from a fan - cy car.

Chorus

On Ju - ly the Fourth, we sing our song a - bout the war fought hard and long. We sing free - dom, we

sing out loud, all to - geth-er, we sing out proud.

Verse 2
The sun is high, it's time to eat!
Here's a blanket, take a seat.
Hot dogs grilling, burgers too.
Plenty of popsicles, red, white, and blue!

Chorus

Verse 3
The sun is down, let's hear the band.
Tap our feet and clap our hands.
A bugler plays her golden horn,
a tune from when our nation was born.

Chorus

Verse 4
Crash! Boom! Bang! Look at the sky,
fireworks exploding up so high.
"What a dazzling show!" we say.
We're glad to be free upon this day.

Chorus

GLOSSARY

announcement—an important thing to say

bugler—a person who plays a musical instrument called a bugle, which is like a trumpet

colonists—a group of people who moved together to a new country

dazzling—bright and showy

exploding—bursting loudly

GUIDED READING ACTIVITIES

1. What ideas do we remember on the Fourth of July? Why are these ideas important?

2. The Fourth of July is about freedom. What is one new way you can learn about freedom in your world?

3. Picnics, parades, and fireworks are all part of celebrating the Fourth of July. Invent a new Fourth of July activity. Explain your activity and why it would be fun for the Fourth of July.

TO LEARN MORE

deRubertis, Barbara. *Let's Celebrate Independence Day.* Minneapolis: Kane Press, 2016.

Kawa, Katie. *The Declaration of Independence Wasn't Signed on July 4th: Exposing Myths about Independence Day.* New York: Gareth Stevens, 2017.

Ponto, Joanna. *Independence Day.* New York: Enslow, 2016.